SOUL WINNING MADE SIMPLE
A Step By Step Guide To Personal Evangelism

LAWRENCE OJI

COVENANT PUBLISHING

Soul Winning Made Simple
Lawrence Oji

Unless otherwise stated, all scripture quotations are taken from the Holy Bible, New King James Version (NKJV). Other versions cited are NIV, KJV, GNB, God's Word, MSG, LEB and NLT.

ISBN 978-1-907734-08-3
First Edition, First Printing May 2016

No part of this publication may be produced, distorted or transmitted in any form or by any means, including photocopying, recording or other electronic or mechanical methods, without the prior written permission of the publisher, or except in the case of brief quotations embodied in critical reviews and certain other non-commercial uses permitted by copyright law.

For permission requests, write to the publisher, addressed "Attention: Permission Coordinator" at the email address below:

Covenant Publishing
samadewunmi@btinternet.com

Covenant Publishing is part of New Covenant Church
Charity Registered in England & Wales number 1004343
Registered Address: 506-510 Old Kent Road. LONDON SE1 5BA

Copyright © May 2016, Lawrence Oji
All rights reserved

Cover Design by Covenant Publishing Team
Published by Covenant Publishing
Printed in the United Kingdom

TABLE OF CONTENT

Foreword - Rev. Mrs Kate Jinadu   v
Foreword - Rev. Tayo Arowojolu   vi
Acknowledgement   ix

Chapters

Introduction: Who Is Jesus?   11
One: Evangelism Postcode - W5 1H   23
Two: The W5   53
*W1 - **WHAT** is Evangelism?*   53
*W2 - **WHO** Should Evangelise?*   57
*W3 - **WHY** Evangelise?*   60
*W4 - **WHERE** Should Evangelism Take Place?* 69
*W5 - **WHEN** Is The Best Time To Start?* 79
Three: HOW - Should We Evangelise?   81
Four: Guidelines For Personal Evangelism 113
Prayer of Salvation   127
Meet Evangelist Solution   129

FOREWORD

Lawrence Oji is a man on a mission. After several years of drug taking and prison sentences there came a day when he experienced a radical, dynamic, life changing encounter with the Lord Jesus Christ.

Having experienced the depths of degradation and despair, his life was turned around. He became a "new creation in Christ." "old things passed away and everything became new" for him.

Lawrence is a man excited about Jesus and His power to transform lives. In this, his second book, he shares His passion with you, the reader. It's passion that pulsates through every page – a passion to see other lives transformed by the love of God. As the Apostle Paul puts it, the "love of Christ constrains him" to obey the Master and to, "Go into all the world…. to tell every creature," the glorious good news of New Life in Christ.

This book will encourage every one of us to become more fervent in soul winning. It is no academic tome. Rather it is vibrant with compelling stories of lives transformed, bodies healed, drug addicts delivered; in fact the whole miracle working pantheon of what the Holy Spirit can do with a man or woman who is totally yielded to Christ.

Here is a man who loves Jesus. Ironically, Lawrence was given the name "Solution" while he was dealing drugs.

How prophetic for a man who is prepared to forgo sleep, to giving of his time, money and energy to introduce dying men and woman to Him who has, and is THE SOLUTION.

I thoroughly recommend this book to all other lovers of the Lord Jesus Christ.

Catherine Jinadu
Pastor New Covenant Church
International President Covenant Women
Founder and Director of Liberty- making people free

FOREWORD

Again Pastor Solution has used this easily digestible book to reach the hearts of readers to convey the heart of Christ - that no one should die as a sinner, and that all may be saved. It is the book for the wise (Proverbs 11:30). I will recommend it as a good evangelism tool that should be used in churches as a 'must have' instrument in spreading and winning souls to Christ.

Rev. Tayo Arowojolu
Pastor, Edmonton Conference
New Covenant Church, United Kingdom

ACKNOWLEDGEMENT

First of all, I want to thank God Almighty for the privilege to be alive to tell my story and to be able to tell others about Him.

Special thanks to you my Pastor, Rev. Tayo Arowojolu for the opportunity you have given me to express my ministry under your own ministry. May the Lord bless you richly.

To every member of the Evangelism team of New Covenant Church Edmonton, I say a special thanks for always being there to support me and ensure there are no gaps during the periods I am not physically available. You have kept the candle burning. You guys are indeed wise.

I thank my beautiful Princesses, Favour Uchechi Abimbola, and Esther Ginikachim Nifemi for going out with me always to evangelise. Thank you also for even going on prison visits with me. I pray that the Lord will call you very early into the ministry and you will answer the call speedily too. You are delectable indeed. I love you loads.

Finally, I want to say a very big thank you to my wife of inestimable value, Stainless Stella, my Angel. It is as though God wanted to really convince me that He loves me dearly, in case sending Jesus to the Cross for my sins didn't make me realise that, so He gave you to me. You are simply the BEST, and the Lord will reward you for being a virtuous wife indeed. Because you fear God, I pray that He will build you houses (Exodus 1:21). I love you, my STAR. With all my craziness for my beloved Arsenal, I am not a fan like you. You are the best fan. You are my number one fan. May the Lord bless you indeed.

INTRODUCTION

JESUS - WHO IS HE?

In my first book, "From Prison To Pulpit", I shared a testimony of how Jesus delivered me from the bondage of drug addiction and prisons on the 21st of March while I was serving another prison sentence for drugs related crime.

Prior to that I had heard songs like, "All powers belong to Jesus", and "At the mention of the name of Jesus every knee should bow", but they didn't make much sense to me until on that fateful day when I had a personal encounter with Jesus and was delivered from the shackles of chain smoking and the life of a jailbird. I remember on that fateful day, I was chain smoking as usual during a timeout from the cell. My cellmate, a guy by the name of Michael asked me, 'Solution, why do you smoke so much?' To which I responded in the usual manner, 'Michael, I cannot stop smoking because I am chained to it. In fact, I will die if I don't smoke for a day, I added. Michael laughed and said, 'that is not true'. I got angry at what I considered his sarcastic remark and began to recount how I had visited the best of doctors in the best of rehabs all over the world and yet no one could help me stop smoking. Michael simply smiled and said that is because you haven't seen the greatest physician – Jesus. There and then, Michael invited me to say a short prayer. Amazingly, every urge to smoke miraculously disappeared and I haven't smoked a single stick of cigarette to this day.

Jesus delivered me! What the best doctors couldn't do, the Lord Jesus did in seconds. There and then, I was determined to share this testimony wherever I go so the world will know that what the Bible says about Jesus having all the powers is not a fable.

Hence, that was what made me write my testimony. I have come to realise too that the world is in the darkness we all witness today because it doesn't know Jesus, and will continually remain in this darkness until Jesus, the Light of the world begins to reign in every man's life.

The question is, how will the world know Him if bible believing Christians don't tell others about Him? Oftentimes, as I have discovered, there are many believers who would want to go out and talk about Jesus but lack the wherewithal to do that effectively.

Hence I thought of how I can simplify the art of evangelism so much that every Christian will not only realise that they are called to evangelise, but also discover for themselves that it is possible to do so. The truth is that we are called to be witnesses of Christ. We have been given everything that we need to meet this great commandment. God will never send anyone on a mission without making a provision. All we have to do is to obey.

BUT WHO REALLY IS JESUS?

I will like to write a short introduction about Jesus for the benefit of those who may not have heard of Him. He is the son of God. He died on the cross of Calvary for our sins.

Jesus while on earth performed many miracles such as healing, casting out demons, walking on water, calming a storm with the command, raising people from the dead, and rising from the dead Himself. Though there have been many great teachers throughout history, none of them have performed such miracles. This is why we can believe Him when He says,

"I am the way, and the truth, and the life; no one comes to the Father, but through Me," (John 14:6).

Therefore, I have purported in my heart to tell people about Jesus wherever I go. Two weeks after my release from Prison in Italy in April 2002, I was in in the city of Padova and on the streets evangelising, telling anyone who cared to listen about Jesus.

When one of my friends, Sunny, who knew me as a junkie noticed that he had seen me for two weeks without a cigarette or the usual company of drug addicts I was used to keeping before my encounter with Jesus, he invited me to lunch in his house. Prior to this time, the likes of Sunny wouldn't want to associate with me for fear of getting into trouble with the police.

Seeing the transformation in my life, he felt safe to extend an invitation. So we agreed a date and time for my visit. On the appointed day, I arrived at his house, knocked on the door and he opened to let me in. He was living in a self-contained apartment, kind of a studio flat, with the cooking area attached to the sitting room. He offered me a seat and set about preparing a meal for me.

We were chatting while he prepared the food. I seized the opportunity to share my testimony. I told him how a guy I met in prison, Michael, prayed with me for less than twenty seconds in the name of Jesus and the urge to smoke left me. I went on to tell him how Michael introduced me to KCM, Europe and I started receiving the Kenneth Copeland victory Magazine and how my faith began to grow from reading these magazines.

When food was served, I noticed that he brought out a syringe with some medication to administer an injection to himself. Out of curiosity, I asked him why the self-injection? He said, 'I am suffering from diabetes. I am on a daily prescription of insulin. When I asked him for how long he was going to be using the insulin for, he said to me that there was no cure for diabetes and that he was going to be using the insulin for the rest of his life.

At that moment, I had a strong urge to tell him about Jesus and His healing power. It was as if the Holy Spirit said to me, "You have been telling him what I did for you, now, I want you to tell him about me, and what I can equally do for him." The moment I heard this, I stopped eating the food and asked my friend if that was what the Word of God said concerning diabetes and sicknesses. I told Him it wasn't the Will of God for us to be slaves to medication as Christ has redeemed us from the curse of the law as written in the book of Galatians 3: 13.

I began to minister to him with scriptures on healing. As I kept speaking to him, he got up from his chair, went into his room, brought out all the syringes and insulin he had in the house and threw them in the trash bin. Then he said to me "Solution, do you know I have never heard it like this before?" I believe that I have received my healing today and I will never need to use insulin for the rest of my life, he added. I prayed with him and led him to Christ there and then in his kitchen, lunch forgotten.

As I write this book in 2016, my friend Sunny, who was told by the doctors that his days were numbered, is happily married with children, totally and completely free from diabetes. This is the same man that was told that he would not have children. Now to the glory of God, wherever I have gone to minister in Italy, he would bring his family to sit under my ministration. Such is the awesome power of our Lord Jesus Christ. Our Lord is faithful. Indeed Jesus is still in the business of healing people.

Another incident that demonstrated the healing power of our Lord Jesus happened in London a year later. As I continued evangelising, telling people about Jesus, the Lord used me as a vessel to heal several other people. As a result, my phone was ringing non-stop. People were calling me to request prayers for all manner of problems and situations that they were going through. One of such was a case of a man whose health had gone so bad, that doctors gave him only a few days to live. For the purpose of this write-up, I will call him Paul. He was HIV positive and this had gone to the stage they call 'terminal'. In response to his call, I set out to visit him at North Middlesex Hospital in London. On arrival at his ward, I met a man who was probably in his thirties, emaciated and looked much older. He was weeping profusely. He was sure that he was going to die seeing that Aids has no cure. Amidst tears, he told me how his wife had abandoned him and made away with their only daughter. He was inconsolable!

Up until now, I had not yet encountered a seeming hopeless situation like the one before me. But I had the assurance that with Jesus, there is no impossibility. Just when I was pondering on what to tell him, I heard the Holy Spirit whisper a scripture to me, Psalm 103. When I opened my Bible and read from verse one to three, He said I should stop and I did so. This scripture says we should bless the Lord who forgives all our iniquities and heals all our diseases. I asked Paul if HIV was a disease and he said yes. Then I said to him that Jesus heals HIV and will heal him. I told him to stop crying.

I prayed with him and led him to Christ on what was supposedly his dying bed. I then got his wife's contact and went to see her. Even the nurse whose table was in front of the room where this patient was, told me she wasn't sure I understood the gravity of his situation. It was obvious she said it in mockery.

After three days, when the nurse saw that Paul did not die and subsequent tests did not show the existence inside him of any HIV virus, she asked to be introduced to Jesus.

To the glory of God, Paul is completely healed to this day. Even as I write this book, Paul is still very much alive. He is fully healed with no trace of the HIV virus and is currently serving as a deacon in another church. He has been to my church, New Covenant Church, Edmonton to worship several times and to share his testimony.

Such is the awesome power of our Lord Jesus Christ.

Jesus is a Healer as written in 1 Peter 2:24 and Matthew 8:17. He is not only a Healer but He is also among many others:

- The Light of the World (John 8:12).
- The Way, The Truth and the Life, according to John 14:6.
- The Door, as written in John 10:9
- The Good Shepherd (John 10:11)
- The Bread of Life (John 6:35).
- The Restorer (John 10:10).
- The Living Water (John 4:14).
- The Word of God (Revelations 19:13)
- The King of kings and Lord of lords (Revelations 19:16).
- The Lamb that was slain (Revelations 5:12 and 13:8).
- The Lion of Judah (Revelations 5:5).
- The burden bearer (Matthew 11:28-30).
- The Prince of Peace (Isaiah 9:6).
- The Peace Giver (John 16:33).

- The Son of God (1 John 4:15, John 10:36).
- The EXACT representation of God (John 1:18).
- He is God (John 1:1, 14, John 10:30-33, Colossians 2:9, Philippians 2:5-11, Hebrews 1:8)

CHAPTER ONE

Evangelism Postcode - W5 1H

We are SOULWINNERS, because that was what Jesus was.

"This is a faithful saying, and worthy of all acceptance, that Christ came into the world to save sinners" (1 Timothy 1:15).

The Bible also says, "The Son of Man is come to seek and to save that which was lost. (Luke 19:10). Jesus came to save sinners. That was and is His mission. First and last, He was a soul winner, and the greatest One the world has ever known.

In the words of T. L. Osborn, "The word Christian means to be like Christ. Jesus came to save people, to seek out the lost. To be called Christians, we are to be soul winners like Him. We are Christ's arms, legs, and mouth on earth, and He wills to do in us and through us what He did when He ministered on this earth. Yet, there are hundreds of thousands of Christians who have never known the joy of allowing Him to win a soul through them."

Theologian Andrew Graystone told Premier Radio, "We are in an age now where what is sometimes called religious literacy is very low." Christians are either reluctant to share their faith or don't know how to do that.

Christians often seem to want God's Spirit to carry the message of His love to lost and hurting people. Church members spend much of their prayer time urging God to do all of the things that He chose them to do which includes visiting the poor and needy, comforting the feeble, blessing and providing for the destitute, encouraging those in prison, sustaining the weak, witnessing to the unbelievers, etc.

How can God's Spirit communicate His message to human persons without a Christian to express Himself through? What can Jesus

Christ do in any town or community without a body to function through? In his book, 'Reaching Your World for Christ', Andrew Murray wrote, "A crucial factor in the evangelisation of the non-Christian world is the state of the church in countries that already have been evangelised. Until there is a more widespread consecration among members of the home church, there can be no hope of expanding the missionary enterprise and making the knowledge of Christ readily accessible to every human being."

The most direct and effective way to promote the evangelisation of the world is to influence Christian workers, and indeed, the whole membership of the church, to yield themselves completely to the authority of Christ as Lord.

Soul winning is an art. The art of knowing where, how, when and what to converse is the Personal Work efficiency. We may possess the Word of God, but if we lack wisdom our efforts will be of no influence and real benefit.

The extent we submit our lives to Christ is the measure of our surrender to Him and to His service.

There is need now more than ever before for the church to seriously set itself to bring the living Christ to a dying world.

We need to ask ourselves how it can be that, our faith in Christ doesn't match our love for Him and for the souls He has trusted us to direct to Him. How can we imagine that our activities were pleasing to God while all the time we were grieving Him by neglecting His last and MOST cherished command, "Go and make disciples of all nations?"

In every culture, the last words of a dying man are always taken seriously, and what is today generally known by Christians the world over as the Great Commission, were the last words of our Lord and Saviour, Jesus Christ, before He died for the world on the Cross at Calvary. Yet, it appears the Church isn't giving it the attention it deserves.

George Verwer, in his book, "Literature Evangelism", describing the state of the church with the greatest assignment the Lord gave the church, wrote, "What is the sense of an architect drawing up blueprints for a house, construction crews building it, decorators putting on final touches only to leave it standing unoccupied?

Likewise, what is the sense of an author writing a book, printers turning it off the press, artists putting an attractive cover on it, if it is only to be stored in a publishing house?" This is more or less the situation existing today in the church, with regards to her attitude towards Evangelism. Why?"

There is always an opportunity to witness Jesus Christ, His love, His companion and His power "anytime" and "anywhere." In my experience, the time is always right. This has been my philosophy as I go about witnessing in different cities that I have had the opportunity to visit. I will attempt to recount a few of the incidents below:

LONDON 2003

"Brother Solution, Brother, Solution, I am tired of living. I want to commit suicide." This was a call I got at about 2.30am in London barely two months after the Lord brought me to my Church, New Covenant Church, Edmonton. I remember being awoken from the dog barking ring tone I was using on my phone then. At first, I thought I was in a dream. The words I heard were exactly those, informing me of an impending suicide bid by a man I had met in church a few days earlier.

Still groggy from sleep, I asked who is on the line. My name is Steve, and I am sure you won't remember my face now but I was one of the people who requested for your contact on the day you came to our Church and shared your testimony. Sleep fled from my eyes. Instantly, I leapt off my bed, firing questions at him and trying at the same time to wear my clothes.

Where are you calling from at this time of the morning, I asked? "Are you at work?" "No," he replied, "I am tired of life and I want to take my life. I am calling from the Thames River Bridge."

I began to plead with him to desist from carrying out such an act. I made him understand that God loves him and has plans for him, and that it was the lies of Satan to make him believe that God hated him and had given up on him.

"Please don't do that," I pleaded with Steve, informing him that as he already heard from my testimony, I too had such thoughts in the past but since I gave my life to Christ, I have discovered that life indeed is sweet. "My partner is sleeping with someone else," he said, "and I don't have any desire to live again." "Forget it," I snapped! "Listen to me, brother Steve," I pleaded. "Good and perfect gifts come from God and you won't have the perfect unless you let go of that which you regard as good."

I kept pleading earnestly and finally he said, "okay, I will not jump yet but what do you want me to do," he asked? "Please take a cab and come to me immediately and the Lord will show us the way out of this," I said. "I don't have any money on me. I wandered away since two days and haven't been home," he said. I quickly promised to pay the fare and waited with bated breath until I heard him say, "okay send your address."

Immediately, I texted my address to him and waited, all the while praying that the Holy Spirit will persuade him to come to me. In the meantime, I sent a text to my Pastor to inform him of what was happening. After what seemed like an eternity, I heard the sound of a vehicle screech to a stop in front of my house. I peeped through the window and saw him come out of the cab. I quickly went outside with my wallet and enquired from the driver what his fare was, settled it and brought him upstairs, to the box room I was living in at the time, where he narrated to me all that he was going through in his relationship. We talked and talked until almost seven in the morning. By the time he left for his house he had become emotionally strong.

God's grace abounded and the unction of God was available to save him through me that morning. I didn't even know where the Thames River was at the time, but the Lord who created the Thames, knew where he was at the time and delivered him from an appointment with an obvious untimely death. It wasn't I that saved him but the Word of God that went forth from my mouth to minister His grace and His love.

I believe that he had the confidence to call me that morning because he was aware of my own testimony. How God delivered me from suicidal thoughts. Thanks to God I have never shied away from sharing my testimonies of how the Lord delivered me from the dungeon of drug addiction, from the cycle of going in and out of prison, and from pangs of depression and suicide attempts that had held me captive for several years. He was about jumping into the Thames River, as he was convinced that God had no love for him and had abandoned him.

I glorify the name of the Lord for the boldness I received from Him to share my testimony the moment He brought me into His church. Not even when a Church Manager at the time tried to dissuade me from letting people know my past life did I budge. Had I swallowed my testimony, how on earth would Steve not have taken his life that early morning? How would Steve have contacted me? How would he have known that Jesus is still setting captives free? God's plan of salvation is to use those whose lives He has transformed to impact other lives.

MILTON KEYNES

One day while on Evangelism at Milton Keynes in the UK, as I was walking with Pastor Ade, who with his wife, Pastor Fola Omotunde, the pastors of the Milton Keynes branch (a suburb of London) of the new Covenant church, I saw a lady who was sat on a pavement by the way we were walking past. She looked totally and completely lost in thought. I approached her with a tract and she cursed and told me off. Rather than letting her reaction offend or put me off, I leaned a bit towards her and whispered in her ears, "You are where I used to be". She angrily asked what I meant by such a remark and I replied her with these words, "You are on drugs, and I too used to be there until Jesus, the great deliverer, delivered me from that bondage." Immediately, her looks and countenance changed, she dropped her guards and became a bit friendly. How did you know I am on drugs, she asked? I replied, the moment I looked at a beautiful lady like you, looking so unkempt and lost in thoughts, I knew you are on drugs. I told her that I wasn't there to judge her but to help her.

I shared my own testimony and encouraged her. She told me that their four children had been taken into care by the Social Services, as her partner, Patrick was equally addicted to drugs and alcohol. She even told me they had tried to receive help from the doctors but unfortunately they got addicted to the substitute drugs; like methadone that was prescribed for them.

I encouraged her to engage the services of the Doctor of all doctors, Jesus Christ, who delivered me from my own addictions. Right there and then I led her to Christ, and before long she started attending our new branch. As I write this, she and her partner, Patrick got married and regained custody of their four children from Social Services.

That was after she went to do her Alpha Course, and the husband went into a Rehab, having also been introduced to Christ through me. Today, she works with an Organisation that helps drug addicts to become free and become what they are here in the world to be according to God's purpose for them when He formed them in their mothers' womb. God has a purpose for every human being. I once heard somebody say that the richest place in the world is not the World Bank, but the cemetery because a lot of people leave this world without actually having lived, and go into their graves with all their gifts and talents intact. The late Dr. Myles Monroe, in one of his last messages, emphasised the importance of disappointing the grave whenever the Lord calls us home. We must die empty. No one should die without having first lived. Our task is to ensure that. And no one lives without Christ. He is the Way and He is the ONLY Way.

Joshua 1:13 says,

"Remember the word which Moses the servant of the Lord commanded you, saying, The Lord your God is giving you rest and is giving you this land

And verse 15 says,

"Until the Lord has given your brethren rest, as He gave you, and they also have taken possession of the land which the Lord your God is giving them. Then you shall return to the land of your possession and enjoy it, which Moses the Lord's servant gave you on this side of Jordan toward the sunrise."

The Bible says,

"For God so loved the world that He gave His only begotten Son that whosoever believes in Him shall not perish but have everlasting life. Goes further to say that God did not send His Son into the world, to condemn the world but that the world through Him might be saved. He who believes in Him is not condemned; but he who does not believe is condemned already, because he has not believed in the name of the only begotten Son of God" (John 3:16, NKJV).

I like the way the way the MSG translation puts it.

"This is how much God loved the world: He gave His Son, His one and only Son. And this is why: so that no one need be destroyed; by believing in Him, anyone can have a whole and lasting life. God didn't go to all the trouble of sending His Son merely to point an accusing finger, telling the world how bad it was. He came to help, to put the world right again. Anyone who trusts in Him is acquitted; anyone

who refuses to trust him has long since been under the death sentence without knowing it. And why? Because of that person's failure to believe in the one-of-a-kind Son of God when introduced to him" (John 3:16, MSG).

From this we know that it is only when Christ is introduced to a person and he fails to believe in Jesus that he receives the death sentence. What if Christ was not introduced to him? Who should introduce Jesus to the world? The Church has received a mandate popularly referred to as the Great Commission, to go into the world and preach Jesus, The Way, to it.

God's desire and plan is that all men shall be saved. The Bible makes it clear in the Book of 1 Timothy 2:3-5,

"For this is good and acceptable in the sight of God our saviour, who desires all men to be saved and to come to the knowledge of the truth. For there is one God and one Mediator between God and men, the Man Christ Jesus."

This is God's plan for the redemption of all, and can only be achieved through us the believers.

It is written in the book of Matthew 28:18-20,

"And Jesus came and spoke to them, saying, 'All authority has been given to Me in heaven and on earth. Go therefore and make disciples of all nations, baptizing them in the name of the Father and of the Son and of the Holy Spirit, teaching them to observe all things that I have commanded you; and lo, I am with you always, even to the end of the age' Amen" (NKJV).

The message translation puts it this way,

Jesus, undeterred, went right ahead and gave His charge: "God authorized and commanded Me to commission you: Go out and train everyone you meet, far and near, IN THIS WAY OF LIFE, marking them by baptism in the threefold name: Father, Son and the Holy Spirit. Then instruct them in the practice of all I have commanded you. I'll be with you as you do this, day after day after day, right up to the end of the age."

The promise is to be with the disciples day after day after day is AS THEY DO THIS. Do what? As they carry out the assignment of Going out and training everyone they meet in a particular way of life.

There is no other organisation in the whole wide world that has been empowered to do this except the church. This is called the Great Commission.

Salvation comes no other way; no other name has been or will be given to us by which we can be saved, ONLY this one, Jesus" (Acts 4:12).

Jesus called Himself THE WAY, (not a way), THE TRUTH and THE LIFE, and that no man can come to the Father EXCEPT by Himself. John 14:6. He called himself the door (John 10:9). In John 10:11, He calls Himself the Good shepherd. When the disciples asked Him to show them the Father, He said to them that whosoever sees Him has seen the Father. The Bible records in John 12:20-21:

Now there were certain Greeks among those who came to worship at the feast. Then they came to Philip, who was from Bethsaida of Galilee, and asked him, saying, sir, we wish to see Jesus" (NKJV).

In Mark 1:35-37, we read:

Now in the morning, having risen a long while before day light and departed to a solitary place; and there prayed. And Simon and those who were with Him searched for Him. When they found Him, they said to Him, "Everyone is looking for You."

It is really necessary for Christians to know that what the whole world is in search of is Jesus, the Prince of Peace. He says in John 14:27, My Peace I give to you, and not the way the world gives it. The drug addict is in search of peace. The alcoholic is in search of peace. The politician that is stealing all the money meant for the masses welfare is looking for peace. Peace cannot be found anywhere unless one has Jesus living inside of them by His Spirit, because He is the Prince of Peace. The world can only find

Him through us His followers. He reconciled us to God and has given unto us the ministry of reconciliation. Unfortunately most of us have become judgemental towards the same world He has commanded and commissioned us to go and reconcile to Himself. The book of Romans 10:14-15 says,

"How then shall they call on Him in whom they have not believed? And how shall they believe in Him of whom they have not heard? And how shall they hear without a preacher? And how shall they preach unless they are sent? As it is written: "How beautiful are the feet of those who preach the gospel of peace, who bring glad tidings of good things!"

It is a grave mistake to think that things will just get better without Christians going out to train people in the way of life that Jesus has commanded and commissioned us. In every human there is the desire to do evil, and until a man's heart is regenerated he doesn't have the capacity to think godly thoughts. No one can have the mind that is in Christ until he is born of the Spirit of God Himself. The world cannot be born of that Spirit if they have no encounter with him. Unless we go, God will not do, for we are His hands and His legs here. We are Christ's ambassadors, and whatever we allow remains, while those things we bind, God will bind. Such is the enormity of the Christian's responsibility, the Christian's authority. The Bible makes it clear that it was to destroy the works of Satan that the Son was made manifest (1 John 3:8). Jesus Himself says in John 10:10 that the thief comes to kill to steal and to destroy but that He came that we may have life and have it in abundance. In Luke 4:18, He says,

"The Spirit of the Lord is upon Me, because He has anointed Me to preach the gospel to the poor; He has sent Me to heal the brokenhearted, to proclaim liberty to the captives and recovery of sight to the blind, to set at liberty those who are oppressed; to proclaim the acceptable year of the Lord."

Peter in Acts 10:38 records,

"How God anointed Jesus of Nazareth with the Holy Spirit and with power, who went about

doing good and healing all who were oppressed of the devil, for God was with Him."

Oftentimes, the devil has cheated people and made them believe in the lies that whatever problems, challenges or trials they are facing is caused by God. Luke 22:31-32 makes us understand that Satan's plan is to take us and sift us as wheat but Jesus has already prayed for us so that our faith will not fail us, but we should encourage others after we have been delivered from such challenges. How can we encourage others if we fail to share our own testimonies?

WITNESSING IN THE MARKET

In May 2005, as I was shopping in Dalston market, a thriving African market in North London with one of my aunties, sister Comfort. I left her in one shop and walked into the very next shop, where I met a lady who was begging for food. She had taken some foodstuff and had no money to pay for the items. I was moved with compassion and I decided to pay for her. Then I noticed that she was just laughing and laughing without any reason or purpose. I didn't know who she was but I just decided to pay for her food because I didn't like the way she was being messed up when I entered that shop.

As soon as I paid for her food, sister Comfort came to meet me in that shop and on sighting this lady, she gripped me and said to me, "Can this be real, or was she in a trance?" This is Patience, the lady who used to drive her and others in her car and take them to our Town's Meeting several years back. Patience had become a mad woman. There and then I decided to end our shopping spree for the day and determined to drive back to the church with her and Patience so I could pray for the lady in the Church. I drove them back to the church and prayed for her, after which I took her to Clapton where she told me she lived. The house was so unkempt and only God knows how long before that day she had slept in that flat.

As is usual with the devil, just like the hen that jumps up and down after the head has been cut off, after I left, the spirit of insanity troubled the woman beyond what she had experienced prior to then and the Police saw her on the road and took her to Homerton Hospital Mental section in Hackney. As God may have it, I had slipped my complimentary card into her pocket before dropping her off.

A nurse in the ward, who happened to be a believer, saw the card and left me a message on my mobile phone regarding the lady. That was how I went to visit her there and prayed for her again, and the Lord healed her and after two days she was discharged and till today, in 2016, as I write this book, she is healed and remains healed. Through her I was introduced to another woman who for two years was paralysed and while praying for this her friend, the Lord showed up and she too was healed. The Bible tells us in the book of Romans that the world has been waiting earnestly for the revealing of the sons of God (Romans 8:19). Brethren, the world is waiting for us. If we don't make a move the world will remain in their bondage. Without God we cannot, but without us, God won't.

The woman trader who messed the mad lady up because of her state then, later received Christ through me a few years later when she saw what the Lord did.

HOSPITAL

A few years ago, a member of my Church sent me a text at about 2am, informing me that her father was rushed to the hospital on his 70th birthday and requested I prayed for him over the phone. When I inquired to know where she was, I was informed that they were at the QE2, at Woolwich. I said to her I was on my way. She was surprised I could leave my house at that hour of the night. Thanks to God, travelling at night in London is not as dangerous as it is in some other countries.

My wife decided to accompany me as she has always done, being my number one fan and the greatest supporter in my ministry. I sent a text message to my senior Pastor informing him of my movement as I always did. He instructed I kept him abreast of the development which I carried out to the letter.

When we got to the hospital about an hour or so later, I was met with a crowd of this sister's family members and the hospital doctors and nurses who were all anxiously waiting for the reply to an email of the man's brain that had been sent by scan to the "best" brain surgeon in the UK, whose office was at King's College hospital. Everyone was waiting. The whole atmosphere was quite tense. If the doctor decided that the man had any percentage of survival, it didn't matter how slim, an air ambulance which they had standby will take him to King's hospital to be seen by the specialist brain surgeon, but if he said there was no possibility, then that was it. While we were waiting, the doctor whose assignment was to keep an eye on the computer, looked up at us and said, "I am sorry, I have a pretty bad news for you guys". The expert had looked at the scan and decided that there was no chance of survival.

The wailing that erupted from the sick man's children and relatives cannot be described. By the grace of God, that didn't move me. I felt the Holy Spirit say to me, "You can't come here and just go back because of this bad report, and otherwise how will these people know that I sent you here?" I walked over to the bed where the man was laid, and even though he looked like a dead man by all standards, I courageously laid hands on him and asked God to show up and heal him. By the time I finished and walked towards the other people standing there in the room, the doctors and the experts there mocked me, wondering if I didn't understand that the best brain surgeon in the UK had said there was no chance of him surviving. I encouraged the family and assured them that the man's situation was not impossible with God and that they should stop crying. When we left the hospital at about 5am, I sent a text to the Pastor to inform him of the situation. My wife said to me that the moment I laid my hands on the man, the machines attached to his body began to vibrate as if there was an earthquake.

I didn't realise that though as I was not the one actually doing the work. I only made myself available for the Lord to do His work through me. We got home at about 6am and slept. When I woke up at about 11am, I saw a text message from the sister telling me that her father scaled through the night into the new day, and I responded him with, "Praise God"! I forwarded her text to my Pastor. At about 4pm on the same day, I got a call from her informing me that the father woke up and asked for food, and when they gave him something liquid and light, he rejected it, saying that he preferred to have something solid.

That was how I decided to go back to the hospital and discovered that God had indeed healed him. When he thanked me for healing him I told him that it wasn't I who healed him but Jesus. The world needs to understand that with God, NOTHING shall be impossible, and that what to men is considered impossible, is possible with God. It is easy for man to give up on man but Jesus will never give up on anybody. There and then in the hospital ward, a medical doctor and a nurse requested to meet this Jesus and I led them to Christ. Hebrews 11:2 says that through faith, the elders obtained a good report. The world needs to know that the Bible is true.

IN A BRAZILIAN JAIL

In the year 2007, I had gone to Sao Paolo, in Brazil for ministry work, where I spent six weeks ministering in Churches and in various prisons, four male prisons and two female prisons. In one of the female prisons, a warder who is also a believer told me of a woman who was jailed for killing her husband and his best friend after her husband found out that she had slept with his friend. Everyone in that prison was avoiding her like a plague as though the crime that brought them to jail was lighter. Nobody showed her any compassion; she was all alone in her solitary confinement.

Once the warder told me about her, I requested that she be brought to me. As she was sent for, the rest of the women prisoners there to hear me minister, all gave her way to come forward, not wanting to have any sort of contact with her. Such was the level of hatred towards her. It was reminiscent of the story of the woman with the issue of blood in the book of Mark 5, where to avoid her touching them because she stank; they provided her free access to the Saviour. When this woman stood before me, I told her that Jesus loved her. That was in September 2007. She told me through an interpreter that she killed two people, her husband and his friend and that I must have been out of my mind to tell her that she was still loved by Jesus.

When I told her how the Lord had picked me up from the gutters, dry-cleaned and sent me to people like herself who the world had no place for, and would do the same for her if only she would receive Him into her life, she wept as I led her to Christ. I was glad to hear that after two years, she was released to a Charity that looked after women who had problems with their husband, as a volunteer. Her life had been transformed. She began to counsel others. Such is the love of Jesus. He always says, "I don't condemn you, but go and sin no more". What He did for the woman who was caught in the act of committing adultery, (John 8), He is still doing even today. He never changes. This is the message the world is waiting to hear from us.

Through Evangelism Postcode, W5 1H, my expectation and hope is that every obstacle and confusion regarding the Great Commission would be exposed and eliminated. What is a postcode? In the UK, the importance of a postcode cannot be over emphasised. A postal code (also known locally in various English-speaking countries throughout the world as a postcode, post code, Eircode, PIN Code or ZIP

Code) is a series of letters and/or digits, sometimes including spaces or punctuation, included in a postal address for the purpose of sorting mail, and locating an address. Postcodes are also being used increasingly by personal navigation devices and online mapping services as a really simple and short way of identifying locations.

Let's now take a look at the W5 (5Ws). It involves the following:

WHAT is evangelism?

WHY evangelise?

WHERE should evangelism take place?

WHEN is the best time to evangelise?

WHO should evangelise?

CHAPTER TWO

The W5

W1 - **WHAT** IS EVANGELISM?

A. Making the unsaved aware of the fact that he is spiritually dead and a child of Satan, making him also realise that it is not his fault, and showing him that God has adequately provided a perfect redemption from that condition, is Evangelism. We must very kindly show him that although it is not his fault that he is in this condition, it does become his fault if he remains in it after he has been shown the Way whereby he can become a child of God.

B. Evangelism is the preaching of the Christian Gospel or the practice of relaying information about a particular set of beliefs to others with the intention of conversion.

The Bible says in the book of Acts of the Apostles 4:20,

"For we cannot but speak the things which we have seen and heard."

2 Timothy 2:2-3 says,

"And the things you have heard from me among many witnesses, commit these to faithful men who will teach others also. You therefore must endure hardship as a good soldier of Jesus Christ" (NKJV).

NLT puts it this way,

"You have heard me teach things that have been confirmed by many reliable witnesses. Now teach these truths to other trustworthy people who will be able to pass them on to others. Endure suffering along with me, as a good soldier of Christ Jesus."

Evangelism therefore means passing it on. As we have received we are asked to tell others. If we have received and refuse or fail to tell others, we are in disobedience and the Lord frowns at every act of disobedience. As a matter of fact, Jesus says in John 14:15,

"If you love Me, obey my commandments".

In John 15:14, He says,

"You are My friends if you do what I command."

In 1 Samuel 15:22, Samuel said,

"What is more pleasing to the Lord: your burnt offerings and sacrifices or your obedience to His voice? Listen! Obedience is better than sacrifice, and submission is better than offering the fat of rams."

Acts 5:32 says that He gives the Holy Spirit to those who obey Him. Joshua 1:16-18 says,

"We will do whatever you command us, and we will go wherever you send us. We will obey

you just as we obeyed Moses. And may the Lord your God be with you as He was with Moses. Anyone who rebels against your orders and does not obey your words and everything you command will be put to death. So be strong and courageous."

Evangelism Is Key

No ministry in the Church is more vital than evangelism. It is telling or spreading the Good News. I love to call it GOSSIPPING THE GOSPEL. Evangelism is alerting people of the reign of God and directing them how to avert His wrath by repenting of their sins and turning to Him. Christians who spread the Good News of the reign and imminent return of Jesus Christ are known as Evangelists, whether they are in the home or living as missionaries away from home. There is nowhere in the Scriptures that you find the word Evangelism, rather the word evangelist is used only three times in the Bible.

"The next day we who were Paul's companions departed and came to Caesarea, and entered the house of Philip the evangelist" (Acts 21:8).

"And He Himself gave some to be apostles, some prophets, some evangelists, and some pastors and teachers" (Ephesians 4:11).

"But you be watchful in all things, endure afflictions, do the work of an evangelist, fulfil your ministry" (2 Timothy 4:5).

Although there is no mention of the word Evangelism in the Scriptures, doing the work of an evangelist means doing evangelism, and no matter what one's ministry may be, he cannot fulfil that unless he does the work of an evangelist. That is why I say that evangelism is key to the fulfilling of anyone's ministry.

W2 - **WHO** SHOULD EVANGELISE?

The best way to answer this question is to narrate the story I will title "IT DOESN'T CONCERN ME"

Once upon a time, a woman went to the market and bought a rat trap because rats were causing havoc in her kitchen. As she was unpacking her bag, the rat noticed that the woman had bought a trap to catch it whenever it ventured into her house to steal food from her kitchen. The rat quickly went to the woman's hen and asked the hen to kindly stand with it in an agreement prayer so that the woman would forget to set up the trap that night. The hen looked scornfully at the rat and said to the rat, "It doesn't concern me." The rat went to the goat and made the same request, but like the hen, the goat said too, "It doesn't concern me" and went away.

Finally the rat ran to the cow, who also said to it, "It doesn't concern me." Disappointed, the rat warned its little ones not to venture near the woman's kitchen unless they were prepared to die. As nobody prayed with the rat, the woman did not forget to set the trap. In the middle of the night, a poisonous snake was caught by its tail by the trap, and the woman heard from her room that the trap had gone off. Hoping it had caught a rat, quietly groped to the kitchen, and was bitten by the snake. Her shout of pain woke her husband who rushed her straight away to the hospital where she was administered an injection, with the express instruction from the doctor to drink pepper soup in other for the injection to work effectively. On arrival from the hospital, the hen became the first casualty. On hearing what happened to their kinswoman, her relatives and friends came visiting to commiserate with the family, and in order to entertain them, the goat was slaughtered.

Unfortunately, the woman died and for her funeral, the last casualty was the cow. Eventually, all those who thought the rat trap wasn't a threat to them and felt it didn't concern them paid with their lives.

This is the attitude of majority of the Christians when it comes to evangelism. So, I say that evangelism concerns everyone. The Bible states clearly that Jesus died on the Cross in order to reconcile us to God and has given to us the ministry of reconciliation (2 Corinthians 5: 17-20).

We are Christ's ambassadors.

He Himself gave the command to His disciples in (Matthew 28:18-20).

Mark 16:15-16 says,

"Go into all the world and preach the Gospel to every creature. He who believes and is baptised will be saved; but he who does not believe will be condemned."

Christ's love is experienced through His Church, through the believer (John 13:34-35).

W3 - **WHY** EVANGELISE?

It is a command from the Master Himself. In the book of Matthew 28:18-20, Jesus said,

"I have been given all authority in heaven and on earth. Therefore, go and make disciples of all the nations, baptising them in the name of the Father and the Son and the Holy Spirit. Teach these new disciples to obey all the commands I have given you. And be sure of this: I am with you always, even to the end of the age" (NLT).

Chapter Two: The W5

A servant doesn't rationalise when his master asks him to do anything. If indeed we are God's servants, we will not try to reason why we should carry out a command.

In Luke 24:49, Jesus said,

"Behold, I send the promise of My Father upon you; but tarry in the city of Jerusalem until you are endued with power from on high."

Then in Acts 1:8, He made it clear to His disciples the essence of that power they were to receive:

"But you shall receive power when the Holy Spirit has come upon you; and you shall be witnesses to Me in Jerusalem, and in all Judea and Samaria, and to the end of the earth".

Being endowed by the Holy Ghost and endued with his power is for the purpose of evangelism. In Acts 4:23-31, the disciples prayed for boldness, and when they were filled with the Holy Spirit, they spoke the word of God with boldness. The power we receive is to enable us evangelise and spread the word, for God wants all men saved.

In Joel 3:14, the Bible tells us that they are multitudes in the valley of decision. A lot of people are confused. There are at the crossroad and don't know what to do or where to go. Some have turned to drugs, while some have turned to gambling. Others have turned to robbery and others yet have turned to dead gods, all in search of peace. The book of Isaiah 13:1-9 describes it as follows:

"Isaiah son of Amoz received this message concerning the destruction of Babylon: Raise a signal flag on a bare hilltop. Call up an army against Babylon. Wave your hand to encourage them as they march into the palaces of the high and mighty. I, the Lord, have dedicated these soldiers for this task. Yes, I have called mighty warriors to express my anger, and they will rejoice when I am exalted." Hear the noise on the mountains! Listen, as the vast armies march! It is the noise and shouting of many nations. The Lord of Heaven's Armies have called this army together. They come from

distant countries, from beyond the farthest horizons. They are the Lord's weapons to carry out his anger. With them he will destroy the whole land. Scream in terror, for the day of the Lord has arrived - the time for the Almighty to destroy. Every arm is paralyzed with fear. Every heart melts, and people are terrified. Pangs of anguish grip them, like those of a woman in labour. They look helplessly at one another, their faces aflame with fear. For see, the day of the Lord is coming - the terrible day of His fury and fierce anger, the land will be made desolate, and all the sinners destroyed with it."

The Lord makes it clear in His word that He takes no pleasure in the death of the wicked.

James 5:20 says,

"Let him know that he who turns a sinner from the error of his way will save a soul from death and cover a multitude of sins".

The Bible says in 1 John 4:20,

"If someone says "I love God", and hates his brother, he is a liar; for he who does not love

his brother whom he has seen, how can he love God whom he has not seen?"

"For the time has come for judgement to begin at the house of God; and if it begins with us first, what will be the end of those who do not obey the Gospel of God? Now if the righteous one is scarcely saved, where will the ungodly and the sinner appear?" Therefore let those who suffer according to the will of God commit their souls to Him in doing good, as to a faithful Creator" (1 Peter 4:17-19).

Beloved, Evangelism is doing good and has its challenges, but without us, God won't and without God we can't.

Soul winning causes our own light to shine perpetually. Daniel 12:3 says,

"Men and women who have lived wisely and well will shine brilliantly, like the cloudless, star-strewn night skies. And all those who put others on the right path to life will glow like stars forever" (AMP).

Soul winning beautifies us.

"But how can people call for help if they don't know who to trust? And how can they know who to trust if they haven't heard of the One who can be trusted? And how can they hear if nobody tells them?" (Romans 10:14 MSG).

"And how will anyone go and tell them without being sent? That is why the Scriptures say, "How BEAUTIFUL are the feet of messengers who bring good news" (Romans 10:15 NLT).

The Gospel is the Good News and by sharing it, our feet and indeed our entire lives become more beautiful. Glory to God!

Another reason why we should win souls is so that we can provoke a party in heaven. Luke 15:10 says,

"Even so, I tell you, there is joy among and in the presence of the angels of God over one (especially) wicked person who repents (changes his mind for the better, heartily amending his ways, with abhorrence of his past sins"

Ezekiel 18:23 and 18:32, says,

"Do you think that I like to see wicked people die? Says the Sovereign Lord. Of course not! I want them to turn from their wicked ways and live.

God makes it clear why we were saved in the first place. Isaiah 49:8-9,

"Thus says the Lord, In an acceptable and favourable time I have heard and answered you, and in a day of salvation I have helped you; and I will preserve you and give you for a covenant to the people, to raise up and establish the land (from its present state of ruin) and to apportion and cause them to inherit the desolate (moral wastes of heathenism, their heritages), Saying to those who are bound, Come forth, and to those who are in (spiritual) darkness, Show yourselves (come into the light of the Sun of righteousness). They shall feed in all the ways in which they go, and their pastures shall be

(not in deserts, but) on all the bare grass-covered) hills" (AMP).

Malachi 4:2 makes it clear that this Sun of righteousness we have been commanded to direct the lost to, is Jesus Christ, the Healer.

What will be the consequence for failure to carry out this assignment?

The answer is in the same book of Ezekiel.

"Son of man, I have made you a watchman to the house of Israel; therefore hear the word at My mouth and give them warning from Me. If I say to the wicked, You shall surely die, and you do not give him warning or speak to warn the wicked to turn from his wicked way, to save his life, the same wicked man shall die in his iniquity, but his blood will I require at your hand. Yet if you warn the wicked and he turn not from his wickedness or from his wicked way, he shall die in his iniquity, but you have delivered yourself" (Ezekiel 3:17-19).

This in my opinion is scary enough to get us started even before getting to the end of this book?

Proverbs 4:7 says that wisdom is the principal thing and in all your getting, get understanding. Proverbs 8:11-12 says,

"For wisdom is better than rubies, and all the things one may desire cannot be compared with her, I, wisdom, dwell with prudence, and find out knowledge and discretion."

What those two scriptures say is that there is absolutely nothing on earth that can match wisdom. James 1:5, says,

"If any of you lacks wisdom, let him ask of God, who gives to all liberally and without reproach, and it will be given to him."

Proverbs 24:3 says,

"Through wisdom a house is built, and by understanding it is established."

No one can start anything without wisdom. It is the basis or rather the foundation of whatever one would build on. However, the easiest way to acquire this wisdom is by winning souls. Proverbs 11:30, says,

"The fruit of righteousness is a tree of life, and he who wins souls is wise."

The opposite of wise is fool. Psalm 14:1 says this,

"The fool says in his heart, there is no God".

Anyone who is not wise is a fool and is also saying in his heart that there is no God. A believer who refuses to carry out this Great Commission of Christ is simply saying there is no God and therefore is a fool because he isn't wise.

W4 - **WHERE** SHOULD EVANGELISM TAKE PLACE?

The answer is, EVERYWHERE.

In Acts 1:8, Jesus said,

"And when the Holy Spirit comes on you, you will be able to be my witnesses in Jerusalem,

all over Judea and Samaria, even to the ends of the world" (MSG).

In Luke 14:21-23, the Bible records this;

"The servant returned and told his master what they had said. His master was furious and said, "Go quickly into the streets and alleys of the town and invite the poor, the crippled, the blind, and the lame." After the servant had done this, he reported, "There is still room for more." So his master said, "Go out into the country lanes and behind the hedges and urge anyone you find to come, so that the house will be full" (NLT).

Brethren, is the house full yet? Why are we not going out? The order is, "Go out". Why are we sitting comfortably in the church when the instruction is, "Go out?" Evangelism is not inside the church but outside the church. Jesus said,

"And the Good News about the kingdom will be preached throughout the whole world, so

that all nations will hear it; and then the end will come" (Matthew 24:14).

Only when everyone has been preached to will the end of all the troubles the world is facing at the moment, come.

Paul was put in jail for preaching the Good News, and rather than being cowed, he continued his message right there and when he saw the result, he wrote this letter to the saints in the church in Philippi;

"I want to report to you, friends, that my imprisonment here has had the opposite of its intended effect. Instead of being squelched, the Message has actually prospered. All the soldiers here, and everyone else, too, found out that I'm in jail because of this Messiah. That piqued their curiosity, and now they've learned all about Him. Not only that, but most of the followers of Jesus here have become far more sure of themselves in the faith than ever, speaking out fearlessly about God, about the Messiah" (Philippians 1:12-14, MSG).

I recall a few years ago when I was visiting a cousin at Victoria, London and my phone rang just as I stepped into his house. The caller was crying and requested I pray for him. I inquired to know what it was he wanted prayers for and all of a sudden he became hysterical and told me he was in hospital and had been given three days to live by the doctors. Apparently he was suffering from what could be termed a terminal disease. When he told me in which hospital he was admitted, without saying exactly what the sickness was, and seeing that he kept crying and couldn't really say anything further, I said to him, "Okay, let me pray for you." He said to me, "Pastor please could you come to the hospital"?

Even though I had a reason for going to my cousin at Victoria, I said to him I would be on my way immediately. I promised my cousin that I would see him on a later date as the invitation to the hospital had taken precedence to my visit to him. On arrival at his ward, it seemed obvious that the doctors could not have been wrong. He also informed me that his wife had abandoned him in hospital and walked away with their only

Chapter Two: The W5

daughter the moment she was given the news of the impending doom.

When I finished praying for him, a lady Nigerian nurse whose desk was positioned right in front of the patient's ward, apparently to monitor him until he would breathe his last, asked me, "Pastor, did he not tell you what the doctors said?" When I told her I already knew, she asked me if just "ordinary" prayer could change all that. I told her that Jesus, the Greatest Healer, was already on his case and that He was going to prove Himself. I and my team in the Evangelism department started visiting him and praying for him. We also made contact with his wife and their young daughter, assisting them the much we were able.

On the fourth day of my visit, seeing that the patient did not die on the third day, the nurse took me into another ward to pray for another patient who also had received his own bad news of a few days to live. This one was from the Caribbean's, and I prayed for him too in presence of the nurses.

To God be the glory, not only were the two patients healed and came to our church, two of the nurses also came and even referred me to several other patients in the same hospital. God is always willing to show us off if only we would show up for the assignment.

Once, I had gone for a Prison visit, and as I was praying for the prisoner who had invited me to that prison, another inmate asked permission from the warder so I could also pray for him. I was to find out that he had never been to any church prior to that but according to him, was fascinated by the way I was counselling the fellow I went to see. I had requested for a Bible from the warders as I was not permitted to take mine inside with me. Amongst the issues the prisoner I went to visit mentioned, I opened the Bible to show him from the word of God that there is a solution to every one of them. Didn't the Bible make it clear in the Book of Revelations 13:8, that Christ was the lamb that was slain even before the foundation of the world?

As we kept on studying the word together, the other inmate got attracted and requested that I minister to him too, which of course I did. There and then, in that Visitors' hall, I led him to Christ. A similar thing happened at an

Chapter Two: The W5

Immigration Removal Centre at Gatwick, where I was invited to speak on the Black History Month. Even though I was not invited to preach, I couldn't hide the fact that I believed in the Master. As I was leaving, an inmate stopped me by the stairs. He was of another faith, but couldn't resist asking me to pray for him as he did not wish to be deported.

I introduced Christ to him, prayed for him and gave him my complimentary card. Only a few weeks after that, I received a call from him. He had been released even though, according to him, he had no one who could help him from being deported. Master Jesus helped him because He does as He pleases and the entire universe is His. Up till now, he goes to Church in Leeds, and could have been part of us in my Church had he been released to stay in London.

And yet another incident that comes to mind is that I was at my place of work one day when my phone rang. The caller was someone I had been inviting to Church for nearly two years but wouldn't come. I had met him at a restaurant a couple of years earlier. Luckily I didn't delete his contact from my phone. This was the first time he would call me as I had always been the one calling him since we met. He was in a serious agony and wanted me to come to his house and pray for him straightaway. I had to choose between the pay I would miss for that day by leaving work before the end of my shift (at this time I was paid on an hourly basis), and saving a soul.

The latter obviously was weightier, so I signed off and left for his house after he texted the address to me. On my arrival, he narrated what his plight, which was quite pathetic. According to him, he returned from Nigeria to the UK only two days earlier, when he started feeling some pains in both feet. The pain was so intense and uncomfortable to the point that he could no longer wear shoes. They began to swell up and were practically bursting and bringing out some fluid. He told me he suspected he had been poisoned at home when he went home for land matters.

I led him to Christ right there in his living room and prayed for him. The Lord healed him. The next day he called to ask for direction to our Church. He still is a full member of the Church since over six years from then. There are always opportunities to introduce the Gospel to people.

There is always someone hurting who Jesus is waiting to touch, and can only reach them through us, for we are His arms and legs here on earth.

Once a woman called to inform me that she couldn't sleep in her house and she was hearing noises in her flat every night, and requested I come to pray in her house. I took a church member and we went there. On our arrival there, I left my friend and the lady chatting in the sitting room while I went to anoint the bedroom, the toilet and the kitchen. When I got back to the sitting room, I assured her she would sleep like a little baby from that night and that I would love to introduce her to Him by whose power I had made the decree, so that she in turn would be empowered to do same for someone else in future. She accepted and right there in her sitting room, I introduced Jesus to her.

The next day she called me to inform me how the night went. She had overslept. She told me she had other things to share which she didn't tell me the previous night. I gave her the Church address and she came to meet me. She had never been proposed to before that day and she was forty that year. That was 2007, and after praying with her, I told her that the Lord was going to surprise her because she believed. By December of that year she got married and subsequently, the Lord made her a mother.

When some months later she called to inform me that the principal of the firm where she worked had refused to pay her and sent her away, I advised she hand the battle over to the Lord standing on a Scripture, James 5:4. What was due to her had been kept by her boss and was crying to God that it was in a wrong account, while herself, the rightful owner of the money, was also crying to the Lord that she had been robbed of her entitlement.

That meant two cries coming to God's ears for the same matter. I was not surprised therefore when she called me one night informing me that her boss called to ask her to come pick up her cheque the following morning and stop torturing him.

Chapter Two: The W5

John 4:34-42 makes it very clear that the harvest is ready. Everyday many people go to hell.

W5 - **WHEN** IS THE BEST TIME TO START EVANGELISING?

The answer is right NOW.

Matthew 9:37-38 says,

"The harvest indeed is plenty but the labourers are very few. Pray ye therefore the Lord of the harvest that He may send more labourers, (or more hands to help), in the harvest."

The time to start is now.

In John 4:34-42, Jesus says that it is a mistake to believe that there is still time to wait before starting. He makes it clear that the field is white already. People are there already and not about to get there: ripe for harvesting. All it takes is to "Look up!" In Joel 3:10, the Bible says that there are multitudes in the valley of decision.. They are in a crossroad to decide which path to follow. Isaiah 13 says it very explicitly that we are the ones to direct them which way they should go. Yes, we are the light of the world. They will go to hell unless we evangelise and direct them to the right path.

When to evangelise is right now. It is not by power or by might but by the Spirit of God. Only He can whisper to our ears saying, "This is the right time." May the Lord anoint our ears to hear Him clearly when He whispers to us in Jesus name, amen.

We now turn to the 1H - The HOW.

CHAPTER THREE

HOW Should We Evangelise?

I dare say that whatever I may present here as the ways to evangelise, will in no way be exhaustive. Therefore, I will first and foremost advice that there is need to be very sensitive to the Holy spirit at all times as He can decide to present us opportunities to win souls at different times and in different circumstances.

In the words of Murray, the First Great Requirement is An Adequate Plan.

In his book, "Evangelism as Jesus did it", David Westlake wrote, "I have got a sneaking suspicion that in the Church today our whole approach to evangelism is out of sync with the model offered us not only by Jesus, but by the early church as well. That word "EVANGELISM", has become so tied up with concepts of pressure, sales, baggage and showmanship that we have forgotten the early lessons handed down from the infant church."

Evangelism has become for some people one of those chores that gets done only when we can't avoid it. The church has placed so many other things ahead of soul-winning, which is the primary assignment the church received from the Master before He left the earth.

Nothing can be more dangerous than to tell people to work if their method of work is not what it should be.

There seem to be two types of evangelism, both of vital importance to the continuing work laid down for us by Jesus. On one hand is corporate evangelism and on the other is personal evangelism. It will be worthwhile to note that the corporate stuff is lifeless and stale unless it works in harmony with the personal evangelism that all Christians have a responsibility towards.

Chapter Three: How Should We Evangelise?

Unlike corporate evangelism which targets huge crowds, Personal evangelism marches to the beat of a different drum, one that connects with individuals, forms relationships and remains in it for the long haul rather than the quick fix. In other words, personal evangelism is all about discipleship. Jesus said, "Go and make disciples."

The Message translation of Matthew 6:7-13 says:

"The world is full of so-called prayer warriors who are prayer ignorant. They are full of formulas and programs and advice, peddling techniques for getting what you want from God. Don't fall for that nonsense. This is your Father you are dealing with, and He knows better than you what you need. With a God like this loving you, you can pray very simply. Like this:

Our Father in heaven,
Reveal who You are.
Set the world right;
Do what is best

As above, so below.
Keep us alive with three square meals.
Keep us forgiven with You and forgiving others.
Keep us safe from ourselves and the Devil.
You are in charge!
You can do anything You want!
You are ablaze in beauty!
Yes. Yes. Yes.

From this one can understand that having zeal to do something must be matched with knowledge of how it is done. Romans 10:1-3, says,

"Believe me, friends, all I want for Israel is what is best for Israel: salvation, nothing less. I want it with all my heart and pray to God for it all the time. I readily admit that the Jews are impressively energetic regarding God – but they are doing everything exactly backward. They don't seem to realise that this comprehensive setting things right that is salvation is God's business, and a most

flourishing business it is. Right across the street they set up their own salvation shops and noisily hawk their wares. After all these years of refusing to really deal with God on His terms, insisting instead on making their own deals, they have nothing to show for it" (MSG).

1 Corinthians 15:3, says,

"For what I received I passed on to you as of first importance: that Christ died for our sins according to the Scriptures" (NIV).

We are required to pass it on just as we received it without diluting it in any form or shape with our own wisdom.

This means that Evangelism and any other assignment that must be carried out for the Lord has to be according to His own terms. It is either done that way or not done at all, else one may run the risk of seeking their own glory rather than God's.

The Bible says:

"So, whether you eat or drink, or whatever you do, do all to the glory of God. Give no offense to

Jews or to Greeks or to the church of God, just as I try to please everyone in everything I do, not seeking my own advantage, but that of many that they may be saved" (1 Corinthians 10:31).

Paul realised that one can easily do things for their own fame while pretending to do it in the name of the Lord. The truth is that the Lord who sees the heart knows our intentions, it doesn't matter how much we pretend. There is no point indulging in anything if we won't do it well. There is a saying, "Whatever is worth doing at all is worth doing well." Evangelism, otherwise known as the Great Commission, is an assignment given to every Christian by the Great God, and if anything should be done well, Evangelism is that, because souls are very important to God hence He sent His only Son, Jesus, to die on the Cross for all so that we all might be saved.

In his book, "Personal Evangelism Course", W. E. Kenyon emphasised the importance of adapting our speech to the people with whom we are dealing. We need to show a real interest in them by our tone of voice and words.

TESTIMONIES ARE POWERFUL TOOLS

One of the ways to evangelise is through our testimonies which in themselves are very powerful tools. Revelations 12:11 says,

"They overcame him by the blood of the Lamb and by the word of their testimonies"

In John 4:28-41 the Bible says this:

"Then, leaving her water jar, the woman went back to the town and said to the people, "Come, and see a man who told me everything I ever did. Could this be the Messiah? They came out of the town and made their way towards Him. Meanwhile His disciples urged Him "Rabbi, eat something." But He said unto them, "I have food to eat that you do not know nothing about." Then His disciples said to each other, "Could someone have brought Him food?" "My food, said Jesus, is to do the will of Him who sent Me and to finish His work. Don't you have a saying, "It is four months until harvest? I tell you, "Open your eyes and look at the fields! They are ripe for harvest.

Even now the one who reaps draws a wage and harvest a crop for eternal life, so that the sower and the reaper may be glad together. Thus the saying, "One sows and another reaps is true. I sent you to reap what you have not worked for. Others have done the hard work, and you have reaped the benefits of their labour."

Many of the Samaritans from that town believed in Him because of the woman's testimony. "He told me everything I ever did." So when the Samaritans came to Him, they urged Him to stay with them, and he stayed two days. And because of His words many more became believers. Our testimonies go a very long way to convict people that there is One who can resolve whatever issues they may be facing in their own lives.

In Acts 26:18, King Agrippa, after listening to Paul's testimony of his encounter with Christ as he journeyed to Damascus with permission and authority to "waste" Christians, said to Paul,

"You almost persuade me to become a Christian." And Paul's response was, "I

would to God that not only King Agrippa, but also all who heard him share that awesome testimony."

The power of our testimonies needn't be over emphasised.

People want evidence that a product works, and our testimonies are the proof they are looking for. If you think you don't have testimonies to share as a believer, to show God's miraculous power in saving to the uttermost all those who come to Him, you have my permission to share mine. I was a suicidal drug addict and jailbird until the Lord set me free from the clutches of the devil and restored all my lost years to me. Glory to God!!

BE HOLY SPIRIT LED

Always remember that you don't preach to convince anyone, but it is the Holy Spirit Himself that convicts people.

One sign that the Holy Spirit is working in a person's life is his or her readiness to learn from the Bible. Argumentativeness disappears, and pride is deflated. Instead of wanting to speak or argue, that person wants to listen in order to learn.

DON'T BE JUDGEMENTAL

Be sympathetic. Never have a "holier than thou" attitude. Even with those who have gone deep into sin, as we call it, we can truly say and feel, "Did not God have great love to send His Son into the world to die for sinners like you and me?"

It is very easy for one to start judging other people who are going through issues in their lives, forgetting that without the grace of God, we are not quite different from those ones. In the Book of Acts Chapter 9:10-18, we read of a disciple of Jesus Christ who was asked by the Lord to go to the house of Judas and pray for Saul so that he would regain his sight, having become blind on his way to Damascus to persecute the Church. The same disciple started telling the Lord why Saul was not qualified to receive salvation. To him, Saul's sins were so grave that forgiveness for him could not be contemplated. What a fallacy!! There is no sin that is greater than another. The Bible says that if we keep all the laws and fail in one, we fail all (James 2:10). It is very important not to forget that it was His grace that cleaned us up.

LISTEN TO PEOPLE

Be a good listener. Let them know that you really care about them. People don't care how much you know until they know how much you care. James 1:19 says,

"My dear brothers and sister, take note of this: Everyone should be quick to listen, slow to speak and slow to be angry."

The devil would not want to lose that soul to you as you try to snatch him from his grips, and therefore can use him to provoke you in other to discourage you from going ahead in your attempt to win him to the Lord.

AVOID ARGUMENTS

Be tactful in your approach. It is very important to have tact in your approach without neglecting the importance of introducing the subject of salvation which is the main purpose of setting off.

> *"Again I say, don't get involved in foolish, ignorant arguments that only start fights. A servant of the Lord must not quarrel but must be kind to everyone, be able to teach, and be patient with difficult people. Gently instruct those who oppose the truth. Perhaps God will change those people's hearts, and they will learn the truth. Then they will come to their senses and escape from the devil's trap. For they have been held captive by him to do whatever he wants"* (2 Timothy 2:23-26 NLT).

> *"Stay away from mindless, pointless quarrelling over genealogies and fine print in the law code. That gets you nowhere"* (Titus 3:9 MSG).

Arguments would definitely lead to quarrelling which will get you nowhere. The Bible says we are not ignorant of the devices of the devil. He will use these to stop one from snatching souls from his grips.

BE PREPARED AT ALL TIMES

Sportsmen who excel in their careers don't just walk into the field without adequate preparation. Know your subject or your topic very well. Master it. This can only happen through preparation.

Jesus the Master Himself had zeal. John 2:17 says,

"Zeal for Your house has eaten Me up".

Paul makes it very clear that zeal without knowledge isn't enough (Romans 10:1-4).

The BEST way to avoid foolish arguments that lead to quarrelling is to be always prepared. That is the only way to stop him in his track. The devil did not take God unawares. Revelations 13:8 says that Jesus was the Lamb that was slain even before the foundation of the world.

1 Peter 3:13-18 MSG,

"If with heart and soul you are doing good, do you think you can be stopped? Even if you suffer for it, you are still better off. Don't give the opposition a second thought. Through thick

and thin, keep your hearts at attention, in adoration before Christ, your Master. Be ready to speak up and tell anyone who asks why you are living the way you are, and always with the utmost courtesy. Keep a clear conscience before God so that when people throw mud at you, none of it will stick. They will end up realising that they are the ones who need a bath. It is better to suffer for doing good, if that is what God wants, than to be punished for doing bad. That is what Christ definitively: suffered because of others' sins, the Righteous One for the unrighteous ones. He went through it all - was put to death and then made alive - to bring us to God."

It is worthwhile to understand that when you go out to evangelise, one needs to be humble and do this with the utmost courtesy. Also it is important to bear in mind that mud will be thrown at you. The scripture says "when mud is thrown at you and NOT if mud is thrown at you". However, we are assured that none of it will stick. Glory to God!!

Do not be afraid to say, "I do not know", when a hard, irrelevant, difficult question is asked you. Do not ever become involved in one of these discussions which would cause you to lose your leading him to a definite decision with Christ. It is better to say, "I do not know", than to give an answer that will confuse him further.

DON'T PUT PEOPLE DOWN

Colossians 4:5-6 MSG,

"Use your heads as you live and work among outsiders. Don't miss a trick. Make the most of every opportunity. Be gracious in your speech. The goal is to bring out the best in others in a conversation, NOT put them down, NOT cut them off."

"Behave yourselves wisely (living prudently and with discretion) in your relations with those of the outside world (the non-Christians), making the very most of the time and seizing (buying up) the opportunity. Let your speech at all times be gracious (pleasant

and winsome), seasoned (as it were) with salt, (so that you may never be at a loss) to know how you ought to answer anyone (who puts a question to you)" (Colossians 4:5-6, AMP).

RIGHT MOTIVE

1 John 4:19-21 should be the reason why we do whatever we do. It says,

"We love Him because He first loved us. If someone says, "I love God," and hates his brother whom he has seen, how can he love God whom he has not seen? And this commandment we have from Him: that he who loves God MUST love his brother also."

Love should be the motive that underlines our mission in soul winning.

It must be the love of Christ that motivates us. We must, at whatever cost learn the reality of verses such as Philippians 2:3:

"Do nothing from selfishness or empty conceit, but with humility of mind let each of you

Chapter Three: How Should We Evangelise?

regard one another as more important than himself. Do not merely look out for your own personal interests, but also for the interest of others."

Without a genuine love for Christ, no one can genuinely love their neighbour. A servant is not greater than his master. Jesus' mission on earth was to die on the Cross so mankind would be saved.

In fact He said in John 15:13,

"Greater love has no one than this, than to lay down one's life for his friends."

If indeed we are Christ like, another person's interest must come before our own.

1 John 3:16 says,

"We know love by this that He laid down His life for us; and we ought to lay down our lives for the brethren."

The Bible says in Philippians 2:21,

"Most people around here are looking out for themselves, with little concern for the things of Jesus" (MSG).

This can basically be summed up in the words, "Not I, but Christ." Not my will, but His! Not my way but His! Not my love, but His! Not my life, but His! In George Verwer's words, When this need is met in our lives, and only then, we will experience God's blessing in our efforts to reach every person with the Gospel of Christ.

BE PASSIONATE

Be patient but persistent. You are dealing with a person whose soul is at stake.

There is need to speak out, telling those around us, what happiness there is in a life spent for Christ and what unfailing strength can be found in Him. Our life need to always echo what Psalm 34:8 says,

"Oh, Come and taste and see for yourself that the Lord is good."

BE COMPASSIONATE

The Bible always records that the Lord was filled with compassion, or that it was compassion that moved Him to do things for people. If we will do what He did, we too should allow compassion to move us especially where people's salvation is concerned.

Jesus lived in rapport with the common people. They were His reason for being in this world. His purpose is our purpose. His mission is our mission. His plan is our plan. He came to save people. We are saved to save people. We are blessed to be a blessing to others.

Apostle Paul was so compassionate about his kinsmen missing out on salvation that he wished that he lost his so they could be saved. Romans 9:1-5. In Romans 10, he fervently prayed for their salvation.

E. W. Kenyon puts it this way, "Always be very courteous and gentle in your speech with an unsaved person. The subject we are handling is a very delicate one. You are pointing out to him the fact that he is a child of Satan. You must be perfectly frank in revealing his condition from the Word of God, yet at the same time you must be very courteous and winning in your manner."

PRAY FOR THE SOULS

Before setting out to tell people about Christ, we ought to have told Christ about the souls. In Psalm 2:8, He says,

"Ask of Me, and I will give You the nations for Your inheritance and the uttermost part of the earth for Your possession."

Oftentimes, we kind of go out and start telling people about Christ without first telling Christ about them. Christ is the only One with the power to turn stony hearts into hearts of flesh. In John 6:44, Jesus says,

"No man comes unto Me, except My Father draws him."

Any attempt to get the job done any other way will prove very difficult, if not impossible, because according to Zechariah 4:6,

"It is not by power, it is not by might but by My Spirit, says the Lord."

Always leave a man with a scripture, and after you have left him, pray that the Word will work in his life.

DON'T CHITTY CHAT

When out to evangelise, if you are in a group of two or more, let your focus be on the souls you are going to witness to. Don't discuss other things. Pray silently as you go along.

DON'T BE IN A HURRY

One man with whom slow, but thorough work has been done, who has taken Christ as Saviour and confessed Him publicly as Lord, is better than a dozen with whom hasty work has been done, and who have not actually been Born Again.

GO OUT! GO OUT!! GO OUT!!!

He NEVER said, "Go and ring a Church bell and pray for people to come." He said, "Go out and find hungry and needy people. Win them, bring them. Compel them to come to the banquet, that My house may be full. Luke 14:23.

And every follower of His did just that. After Christ's ascension, His followers continued doing what He had been doing. They stayed busy witnessing in the markets, on the streets, in houses, at public wells, talking, reasoning, witnessing, persuading, preaching, winning souls, compelling people to believe the Gospel and to come to the kingdom of God.

Jesus took His message to the people. He went wherever they could be encountered, in market places, in streets and roadways, on mountain sides, by seashores, in private homes. He was even criticised for identifying with the kinds of people who needed His love and compassion. The religious leaders complained: "This Man receives sinners and eats with them." Luke 15:2.

Apostle Paul said,

"I am all things to all men that I may win some" (1 Corinthians 9:19-23).

RELATING WITH PEOPLE MUST BE OUR LIFESTYLE

Our everyday actions should become channels through which we can fulfil Jesus' "Great Commission." Our lifestyle is the greatest tool of evangelism. People generally don't care how much you know until they know how much you care. 2 Corinthians 3:2 says,

"For you are the epistle known and read by all men."

There is something special about Jesus: He didn't "DO" things to people: He had a relationship with people." He was so able to connect with people that it was through His relationships with them that He was able to work most profoundly. It is obvious that Jesus' method was so different from our modern day spiritual sales pitch. For Jesus, it is absolutely about relationship. Unfortunately, many in the church have developed selective amnesia when it comes to this point: we may acknowledge that God wants us to develop a relationship with Him, but when it comes to how we treat others, well, that is a different matter altogether. Many of us have become so wrapped up in getting people into the kingdom of God through logic, arguments or threats of violence that we have completely forgotten the relationship model as shown by Jesus Himself.

The game plan that Jesus laid out before His disciples was simple: Go and form relationships with others that are similar to those I have formed with you. Jesus was looking for apprentices, people who were up for becoming like Him through a process of spending time with Him.

D. L. Moody, one of the best known evangelists, was once criticised for the way he did evangelism. Replying about his own evangelistic techniques he said, "Frankly sir, I prefer the way that I do it to the way that you don't. While the more traditional model of evangelism might not work for all of us, at least there are plenty around us who are having a go.

Nobody can give what they don't have. Obviously, we cannot invite others to have a relationship with Jesus if we don't first have a relationship with Him, We cannot say to others,

"Come and taste and see that the Lord is good", (Psalm 34:8) if we haven't first tasted Him.

For many of us however, evangelism has rightly meant imitating Jesus' approach and encouraging others to establish their own relationship with Him. But in an attempt to do the right thing, could we be taking it a little too literally? Perhaps there is room for the argument that, like Jesus, we too need to start out by offering a relationship to others, although making clear that it is a relationship with ourselves too.

If all we do is invite people to have a relationship with Jesus, without any intention of having any relationship with them first, we run the risk of giving off a message that clearly states it is not our intention to become contaminated by contact with ungodly people. "Come and meet Jesus," we proclaim with enthusiasm and joy, "but don't even think about having me like and get to know you."

It is this attitude that can leave those on the receiving of our evangelistic efforts with the feeling that they are just another consumer receiving just another sales pitch, creating the impression like the pumped-up telesales person, all that matters is clinching the deal; the rest is irrelevant.

DROPPING OTHER THINGS

In his book, "Active Evangelism", referring to what happened in Acts of the Apostles Chapter three, Derek Prince wrote this:

Peter and John stopped.. They were intending to go to the temple for regular time of prayer — but they abandoned their plans in order to respond to this man's plea. They avoided the snare of the priest and the Levite in the story of the Good Samaritan who seem to have allowed duty to be their excuse for neglecting an opportunity to help a fellow human being.

Oftentimes, we've allowed even church matters to prevent us from ministering to lost souls on our way to the church.

Looking back, I feel guilty for those times I have been so busy rushing to church meetings that I have not had time to talk to my neighbours who have been ready to chat. Passing the time of day with them, besides building up friendship, so often provides scope for Christian witness. We can sometimes hide behind "Church "or "family" duties so that we fail to seize God-given moments for fostering good relationships.

TRUST IN JESUS POWER AND NOT IN YOURS

The Bible says in 1 Corinthians 3:6,

"Paul plants, Apollo waters but God gives the increase."

Peter's witness was based upon his confidence in Jesus, and the power and authority of His name. "Silver and Gold I do not have, he said, but what I have I give you. In the name of Jesus Christ of Nazareth, walk." Peter suited his actions to his words as he held out his hand to the crippled man. The man jumped up to him – literally, "he leapt like a deer." This was more than a miracle. It was a sign, since a Messianic prophecy foretold,

"Then will the lame leap like a deer" (Isaiah 35:6).

Our own confidence must likewise be in the power and the authority of Jesus and especially in His authority to forgive sins because of His sacrificial death on behalf of sinners. We too must suit our actions to our words. We need to encourage them to trust in Him and prove His faithfulness to His promises. John's seizing of one opportunity led to another. Acts 4:4 records that as a result of this singular act, five thousand others gave their lives. This would not have happened had they not had time for the crippled man in front of the Beautiful Gate.

TAKE THE INITIATIVE

The same way Peter took the initiative and turned to good spiritual account this everyday occurrence of the lame man's plea for help by saying to him, "Look at us!" we also can do the same, if we have eyes to see and ears to hear. People will often say things that we may use to turn their focus away from the material and physical to the spiritual.

A FEW EXAMPLES

"What a frightening state the world is in - how is it all going to end?" What an excellent

Chapter Three: How Should We Evangelise?

opportunity to speak of the return of our Lord Jesus! "Yes, it is frightening; but I am glad God has told us how it is all going to end."

Isn't it dreadful the way inflation increases and how one's money goes nowhere?" Yes, but isn't it good that the best things in life can't lose their value!" "What do you have in mind?" "I mean our health and important things like knowing God."

"There is not much good news - if any - in the newspapers." You are right! There is really only one piece of good news that is for everyone - that is the good news of Jesus Christ,"

Such sample interchanges can sound artificial put down on paper, but spoken naturally and spontaneously, they may be openings for sharing the Good News, the Gospel.

Opportunities that present themselves to share the Gospel may be missed or seized. Oftentimes, they are missed because we are too busy doing other things, caught up with our own affairs.

Opportunities are lost to the lazy, and are captured by the diligent. Paul knew this, and urged his Colossian Christians to pray for him in his own sharing of the Gospel (Colossians 4:2-5).

BE SENSITIVE TO THE SPIRIT AT ALL TIMES

In ordinary everyday circumstances - such as when we move house or when new neighbours move in next to us - God's Spirit may have a hidden purpose. He can order our work relationships for us to bring the Lord Jesus to people who might not otherwise hear about Him. He can organise our travel arrangements so that we sit next to someone to whom He wants us to witness.

Sometimes we may not see what place our witness has had in the life of another person, and yet we may be sure that it was no accident that we were able to share what we did. This was Phillip's in Acts 8:26-40. Of course, we should use the brains God has given us as we plan our evangelism, but we must submit all our thinking to the Holy Spirit. We will find Him placing a burden upon us for people's conversion and prompting us to pray for them. Ideas will come to mind about how best to reach out to them and, as we pray, we will find Him giving us an assurance and a peace about the right approach.

Sometimes He may cause us to focus on a particular individual. Behind the instruction for Philip to leave Samaria was God's saving purpose for one man - an Ethiopian - and through him, probably many others in Ethiopia.. The Holy Spirit caused Philip to be in the right place at the right time.

CHAPTER 4

Guidelines For Personal Evangelism

From Luke's account of Philip's evangelism we can take some guidelines for ourselves.

Philip recognised the value of an individual. He was prepared to speak to just one individual on his own.

He was available to God. He was ready to be and go where God wanted. We cannot expect God-given opportunities for witness if we live disobedient lives.

Philip had learnt to listen and to ask the right questions.

Philip spoke about Jesus rather than about religion.

We must not fall into the trap of seeing any day as "ordinary" or as holding no promise for evangelism.

The success of the apostles in evangelism was as a result of their dependence on the Holy Spirit, just as the Lord promised in Acts 1:8. Those who are active in evangelism are aware of just how much they depend upon Him. The knowledge the early Christians had of the Holy Spirit living with them, and in them, explains how they turned the world upside down for the sake of their Master's kingdom. We can do exactly the same today if only we can rely on Him (John 14:17).

Nobody can be won to Christ unless the Father draws them (John 6:44). The Holy Spirit was behind the number of disciples increasing rapidly and the delightful news of many priests becoming obedient to the faith. As one by one they made the all-important confession, "Jesus is Lord."

Chapter Four: Guidelines For Personal Evangelism

GO OUT

Without a doubt the most effective means of getting Christian literature into the hands of the unsaved is by taking it to them. This is where the bottleneck lies. The evangelistic method of Apostle Paul was not so much a "you-come-to-me" evangelism. He said,

"I have kept back nothing that was profitable unto you, but have showed you, and have taught you publicly, and from house to house" (Acts 20:20).

TEAM UP

Soul-winning is not a competition. It is a collective assignment for all believers, and the word TEAM, means, "TOGETHER EVERYONE ACHIEVES MORE." There is need to pray for one another, support one another and as a matter of fact empower one another. In the words of Corrie Ten Boom, "A wall with loose bricks is not good. The bricks must be cemented together, for the wall to stand." We are all members of the same family and a house that is divided against itself cannot stand (See Matthew 12:25, and Mark 3:25). We must do everything possible to stifle the spirit of unnecessary rivalry that has crept into the body of Christ because in heaven there are no denominations.

In his book, "Wake Up, Team Up!" Pastor Williams Olaniyi, emphasised the essence of unity, by likening it to members of a football team who put on the same jerseys. This at the best is for outward identity, whereas the team can only win when the hearts of the players are knitted for the same purpose, just like the Trinity. It is more dangerous when players are dressed in the same colours but are secretly trying to outplay each other. That way they will only be wasting their time.

It is only when there is unity that the Lord will command His blessing (Psalm 133), and the devil knows it too, hence will try all he can to ensure that Christians are not united in their war against his kingdom of darkness. Deuteronomy 32:30 says,

"How one can put a thousand to flight and two shall chase ten thousand."

Chapter Four: Guidelines For Personal Evangelism

There is strength in unity. Apostle Paul writing to the Christians in Corinth, said thus,

"Dear brothers and sisters, when I was with you I couldn't talk to you as I would to spiritual people. I had to talk to you as though you belonged to this world or as though you were infants in Christ. I had to feed you with milk, not with solid food, because you weren't ready for anything stronger. And you still aren't ready, for you are still controlled by your sinful nature. You are jealous of one another and quarrel with each other. Doesn't that prove you are controlled by your sinful nature? Aren't you living like people in the world? When one of you says, "I I am a follower of Paul," and another says, "I follow Apollos," aren't acting just like people of the world? After all, who is Apollos? Who is Paul? We are only God's servants through whom you believed the Good News. Each of us did the work the Lord gave us. I planted the seed in your hearts, and Apollos watered it, but it was God who made it grow. It is not

important who does the planting, or who does the watering. What is important is that God makes the seed grow. The one who plants and the one who waters work together with the same purpose. And both will be rewarded for their own hard work. For we are both God's workers. And you are God's field. You are God's building" (1 Corinthians 3:1-9 NLT).

Again, he wrote in 1 Corinthians 1:10-13,

"I appeal to you, dear brothers and sister, by the authority of our Lord Jesus Christ, to live in harmony with each other. Let there be no divisions in the church. Rather, be of one mind, united in thought and purpose. For some members of Chloe's household have told me about your quarrels, my dear brothers and sisters. Some of you are saying, "I am a follower of Paul." Others are saying, "I follow Apollos," or "I follow Peter," or "I follow only Christ." Has Christ been divided into factions? Was I, Paul, crucified for you? Were any of you baptised in the name of Paul?"

Chapter Four: Guidelines For Personal Evangelism

Of course not! Without unity in the body of Christ, we will not make any effect. Little wonder why there are churches everywhere, yet darkness is still covering the earth. The division is so glaringly obvious.

A good example of what unity can achieve is the building of the Tower of Babel. In Genesis 11:1-6, we read,

"Now the whole earth had one language and one speech. And it came to pass, as they journeyed from the east, that they found a plain in the land of Shinar, and they dwelt there. Then they said to one another, "Come, let us make bricks and bake them thoroughly." They had brick for stone, and they had asphalt for mortar. And they said, "Come, let us build ourselves a city, and a tower whose top is in the heavens; let us make a name for ourselves, lest we be scattered abroad over the face of the whole earth." But the Lord came down to see the city and the tower which the sons of men had built. And the Lord said, "Indeed the people are one and they all have one language,

and this is what they begin to do; now nothing that they purpose to do will be withheld from them."

We can see that even God said that nothing they wanted to do can be withheld from them, because they were in unity of purpose. Fighting for the same goal; trying to achieve the same result. However, because their motive was the wrong one, (they wanted to make a name for themselves), the Lord had to stop them. Were they building for the right reason, the Lord would not have stopped them. He said in verses 7-9,

"Come, let us go down and confuse their language, that they may not understand one another's speech. So the Lord scattered them abroad from there over the face of all the earth, and they ceased building the city."

This means that the easiest way to stop a people from achieving an objective is to put confusion in their midst. Jesus said in Matthew 18:19-20,

Chapter Four: Guidelines For Personal Evangelism

"Again I say to you that if two of you agree on earth concerning anything that they ask, it will be done for them by my Father in heaven. For where two or three are gathered together in My name, I am there in the midst of them."

The presence of the Lord makes hills to melt like wax (Psalm 97:5). Verse 3 of Psalm 97 says because fire goes before Him to consume His enemies. Therefore if our gathering is unto Him, we are sure that He will walk with us and that makes our work easier and results achievable. Amos 3:3 says that,

"Two cannot walk together except they are in agreement."

The enemy will do everything he can to ensure that we don't walk in unity but we must resist him. Remember, we are going into his camp to take his spoils from him and we don't expect him to give them up easily. He will fight with everything he can to keep the spoils, (the souls in his camp), but we are not ignorant of his devices. Glory to God! Unity is strength. The book of Ecclesiastes 4:9 says,

"Two are better than one, because they have a good reward for their labour."

Results are greater and the reward is higher when we work in unity. In 2 Timothy 2:24-26, it is written,

"And a servant of the Lord must not quarrel but be gentle to all, able to teach, patient, in humility correcting those who are in opposition, if God perhaps will grant them repentance, so that they may know the truth, and that they may come to their senses and escape the snare of the devil, having been taken captive by him to do his will."

The way we can succeed as God's ambassadors to make those in the grips of Satan come to their senses and embrace Christ, which is our assignment as Christians, is to work in unity of purpose, and this cannot be overstated. In John 17:20-23, Jesus said,

"I do not pray for these alone, but also for those who will believe in Me through their word; that they all may be one, as You, Father

are in Me, and I in You; that they also may be one in Us, that the world may believe that You sent Me. And the glory which You gave Me I have given them, that they may be made perfect in one, and that the world may know that You have sent Me, and have loved them as You have loved Me."

Jesus Himself made it clear that the Father, who also has become our Father from the day we received Christ as our Lord and Saviour, loves us just as He loved Jesus. That is why He said in John 20:21,

"As My Father has sent Me, so send I you."

As His mission on earth was to reconcile the lost to His Father, so should our own mission be also (2 Corinthians 5:18-20). This can only be achieved through unity of purpose. United we stand, divided we fall and fail. May we not fail in our assignment in Jesus name, Amen.

SAY IT AS IT IS

Paul wrote in 1 Corinthians 1:17-21,

"God didn't send me out to collect a following for myself, but to preach the Message of what He has done, collecting a following for Him. And He didn't send me to do it with a lot of fancy rhetoric of my own, lest the powerful action at the center - Christ on the Cross - be trivialised into mere words. The Message that points to Christ on the Cross seems like sheer silliness to those hell-bent on destruction, but for those on the way of salvation it makes perfect sense. This is the way God works, and most powerfully as it turns out. It is written, I'll turn conventional wisdom on its head, I'll expose so-called experts as crackpots. So where can you find someone truly wise, truly educated, truly intelligent in this day and age? Hasn't God exposed it all as pretentious nonsense? Since the world in all its fancy wisdom never had a clue when it came to knowing God, God in His wisdom took delight

in using what the world considered dumb - preaching, of all things - in other to bring those who trust Him into the way of salvation" (MSG).

This shows exactly how God intends we disseminate this information to people - say it just as it is. Not with our own wisdom, because the wisdom of man is foolishness unto our God (1 Corinthians 3:19).

BE A GOOD COMMUNICATOR

In the words of theologian Andrew Graystone we are in an age now where what is sometimes called religious literacy is very low. Christians have not always been that great at the way we've presented Christian faith towards other people. We've not always been gracious and winning. Sometimes Christians are offensive. I don't mind if the message of the Gospel is offensive, in fact it ought to be - it upsets people. It will, because as the saying goes, The Truth is always bitter, but must be told. But we, as Christians don't need to be offensive in the way we present it. We need to be gracious and warm and loving, just as the Bible teaches us in Ephesians 4:29,

> *"Let no corrupt speech proceed out of your mouth, but such as is good for edifying as the need may be, that it may give grace to them that hear."*

KNOW YOUR SUBJECT

The greatest mistake one will make is to give a salesman a product he knows little or nothing about to market. There is the tendency that potential buyers would have questions that will demand instant responses in order for them to make up their minds whether to invest their money and time in it or not. The art of selling the gospel is no less demanding than other products. Therefore, before we dare venture on to the streets to do the work of an evangelist we need to know our subject well.

PRAYER OF SALVATION

If you don't know this Jesus and desire to do so, this is your opportunity. Just say this prayer with all your heart:

Dear God, I believe with my heart and I confess with my mouth that Jesus is Your Son whom You sent to the Cross to die for me and You raised Him again from the dead after three days by your Holy Spirit. Lord Jesus, I confess to You that I am a sinner and I repent of my sins. Forgive me and cleanse me with Your Precious blood. Write my name in the book of life. Fill me with Your Spirit. Satan, I reject you from today. You have no power over me again because I am now a child of God. Thank You, Lord for saving me. I am now a new creature. Amen.

If you have prayed this with all your heart, I will advise you look for a Bible believing church and become a member.

In the meantime I am willing to answer your questions and give you more support in your journey of walking with Christ.

My contact is:

Evangelist Solution

Solutionministries2001@yahoo.com

Telephone: +447889080268

MEET EVANGELIST SOLUTION

Lawrence "Solution" Oji was born with the proverbial silver spoon in his mouth. He could have risen to the top echelons of life in his native Nigeria - through the civil service, the military, or the private sector. After a few golden, but squandered opportunities, destiny handed him yet another chance for a fresh start with a university education in New Delhi, India. A star student, he nevertheless managed to plunge into the dark depths of drugs.

Early success in drug dealing quickly cemented his own addiction and fueled a jet-set lifestyle that crisscrossed a nexus of leading cities in Africa, India and Europe. The law caught up with him however, where he became a perpetual prisoner. One day, completely exasperated by his enslavement to drugs and failed suicide attempts, he returned to prison to find that God was waiting for him with arms wide open. It was Lawrence's only hope. It was his last option. The star student didn't fail this time.

Soul Winning made simple is his second book, and true to its title, you will be amazed at its simplicity and practicality to get you started as a soul winner. What a guide!

AUTHOR'S FIRST BOOK

"From Prison To Pulpit"

Lawrence "Solution" Oji was a drug addict and jailbird for several years until the saving power of our Lord Jesus Christ touched him inside a prison cell in Italy and literarily "dry cleaned" him and took him away from the squalor of drugs and prisons and placed him on the pulpit. It is an account of how he has come to discover for himself that with God, nothing shall be impossible. In his own words, "There is no life battered, shattered and scattered that Jesus Christ cannot gather again." It is a book recommended for anyone who is challenged by the merciless power of any form of addiction and is in high demand.

Lawrence has ministered in prisons as well as in drug joints wherever he travels to. Read it and see our God in action even today.

ISBN-13: 978-8897896968

www.ingramcontent.com/pod-product-compliance
Lightning Source LLC
Chambersburg PA
CBHW060807050426
42449CB00008B/1574